Mozart
The Wonder Boy
Study Guide

By Judy Wilcox

eezok
publishing
Elyria, OH

Mozart
The Wonder Boy
Study Guide

ISBN 0-9746505-4-4
© 2005 by Zeezok Publishing

Published by:
Zeezok Publishing
PO Box 1960
Elyria, OH 44036

www.Zeezok.com
1-800-749-1681

Map of the major cities Mozart visited

Mozart's World and Place in Musical History

Middle Ages	450 – 1450
Renaissance	1450 – 1600
Baroque	1600 – 1750
Classical (W.A. Mozart 1756 – 1791)	**1750 – 1820**
Romantic	1820 – 1900
20th Century or New Music	1900 – Present

1756 – 1791

1759 Wolfgang Mozart begins playing thirds on the clavier, all on his own.

1756 Wolfgang Amadeus Mozart is born on January 27, in Salzburg, Austria.

1761 Wolfgang Mozart composes his first piece, a minuet.

1760 Wolfgang Mozart begins taking clavier lessons from his father, Leopold.

1763 The Mozart children's second musical tour is initiated: they travel through much of Europe and England. Wolfgang Mozart's music is first published.

1762 Wolfgang and Nannerl Mozart play for Prince Joseph in Munich and begin their first musical tour by playing for Empress Maria Theresa in Vienna.

1767 Wolfgang Mozart becomes ill with smallpox in Vienna.

1766 The Mozarts return to Salzburg from their second tour, which lasted three years.

1770 Wolfgang Mozart's first opera, *Mitridate*, is produced in Milan, Italy. Wolfgang receives the Order of the Golden Spur, an honorary knighthood given by papal decree.

1769 Wolfgang Mozart travels with Leopold to Italy. Nannerl does not come on this tour.

1772 Wolfgang starts his third musical tour of Italy (through March of 1773). Mozart becomes the concert director for the new archbishop, Hieronymus Colloredo.

1771 Wolfgang begins his second tour of Italy, from August through December.

1778 Wolfgang and his mother visit Paris, where his mother dies suddenly.

1777 Wolfgang Mozart leaves Salzburg to tour Europe and "find a job." His mother accompanies him on this trip.

1782 Wolfgang marries Constance Weber in August.

1779 Wolfgang is appointed composer to the imperial court in Vienna.

1783 Wolfgang makes his last visit to Salzburg.

1784 Wolfgang falls critically ill with what is believed to be complications of a kidney failure. Wolfgang's son Karl Thomas Mozart is born.

1786 Wolfgang's opera *The Marriage of Figaro* is produced in Prague.

1787 Leopold Mozart dies in May. Wolfgang's *Don Giovanni* is produced in Prague in October.

1791 Franz Xaver Mozart is born in July. *The Magic Flute* is produced in Vienna in September. Wolfgang dies in Vienna on December 5.

4

Chapter 1 – Early Days in Salzburg
(1756 – 1761)

Reading Comprehension Questions

1. Why did Father Leopold come bounding up the stairs at the beginning of this chapter?
   - To see his new son, p. 13.

2. The baby was baptized as Johannes Chrysostomus Wolfgangus Theophilus Mozart, but what did his parents usually call him?
   - Wolfgang, or Wolferl, p. 14.

3. Can you name any of the Mozart family pets — by species or by name?
   - A cat, a yellow canary, a puppy named Bimperl, p. 15.

4. What was Papa Leopold's occupation?
   - Court composer and conductor of the court orchestra, p. 16.

5. What did Wolfgang learn to do just by watching his older sister, Nannerl?
   - Play the clavier, p. 17.

6. How did Wolfgang amuse himself for hours on end — to the harm of the wallpaper and tablecloths, unfortunately?
   - By figuring out or doing sums (math problems), p. 20.

7. The Mozart family soon learned that there was one thing Wolfgang enjoyed doing more than anything else — even more than playing with toys. What was it?
   - Playing music, or composing, pp. 17, 20.

8. Whom did Wolfgang love most next to God?
   - Papa Leopold, p. 24.

Character Qualities

Family-Oriented (p. 13) – Leopold was proud of his new son, and Marianne (Nannerl) was glad for a little brother (p. 13). The parents were kind, attempting to do everything they could to make their home a cheerful one (p. 16). Leopold took time to teach his children music, an activity that unified their home, making it a welcoming place (p. 16, 17).

Eager Learner (p. 17) – Wolfgang expressed an interest in learning the clavier just by observing his sister's lessons and experimenting with thirds. He hated stopping his lessons and was earnest in wanting to learn more (p. 19). The young Mozart even attempted to write a concerto (p. 23).

Energetic Enthusiasm (p. 16) – Wolfgang pounded his fists in time to the music, and they had a hard time keeping him away from the clavier (p. 17). His first attempt at composing a concerto was covered with inkblots and smears in his enthusiasm to write down his musical ideas (p. 22).

Sweet-tempered (p. 18) – Wolfgang was described as sweet-tempered and patient. He sat to learn a new minuet, and then cheerfully ran off to find his sister (p. 19). He smiled merrily when Papa talked with him about the gift God had given him (p. 24).

Creative (p. 17) – Finding thirds at the age of three, writing a minuet at age five (p. 21) and a concerto at five (p. 23), all seem to show tremendous creative abilities. And God was praised for this musical gift and creative spirit (p. 23).

Revered His Father (p. 24) – "Next to God comes Papa," young Wolferl announced. His love for his father was evident in how he enjoyed spending time with his father during music lessons (p. 19), in his eagerness to have Leopold write his songs in a copybook (p. 20), and in being unintimidated by his father — even sitting at his father's desk to write a concerto (p. 22).

Tidbits of Interest

Pages 11, 12 – Salzburg is in a valley at the edge of the Alps, with the River Salzach flowing nearby the city. Salt mines near the river gave the city its name. The castle described as "cold and silvery in the moonlight" is the castle of Hohen-Salzburg, built in 1077; it is considered Europe's largest fortification.

Page 13 – The Mozarts lived on the third floor of the "Hagenauer House" for twenty-six years. It was named after its owner, a grocer friend of the Mozarts. Their home consisted of a kitchen, small chamber, living room, bedroom, and a study. Leopold Mozart and Anna Maria Mozart had six children, but only two survived to adulthood. Marianne (or Maria Anna) was four years older than her little brother. Her nickname, Nannerl, is what German-speaking people call a "cozy name" — a name of affection and sweetness, such as Susie is a cozy name for Susan, or Danny for Daniel.

Page 14 – The Mozarts were devout Catholics who had their new son baptized into the church just a few days after his birth on January 27, 1756. He was christened as Johannes Chrysostomus Wolfgangus Theophilus Mozart. The name *Theophilus* means "loved by God," which is translated in Latin as the name *Amadeus*.[1] His parents' religious influence and guidance seems to have developed within him a personal relationship with Christ and a deeply religious nature.[2] He once wrote his father, "Papa must not worry, for God is ever before my eyes. I realize His omnipotence, and I fear His anger; but I also recognize His love, His compassion, and His tenderness towards His creatures. He will never forsake His own. If it is according to His will, so let it be according to mine. Thus all will be well and I must needs be happy and contented."[3]

Page 15 – Wolfgang loved animals. He even once broke off a concert to chase after a cat that had wandered into the hall. He also wrote his terrier, Bimperl, notes of affection from cities all over Europe.[4]

Page 16 – Leopold Mozart was the assistant music director of Archbishop Sigismund von Schrattenbach's chapel in Salzburg.

7

In this role, he wrote music and directed the court orchestra for the archbishop. Archbishop Schrattenbach was a man who encouraged music and the arts — even keeping a permanent orchestra of twenty-one to thirty-three musicians.[5] He was very "well disposed towards the Mozart family," allowing Leopold leaves of absence for concert tours and training.[6] Leopold authored a well-known book on violin playing (actually published the same year as Wolfgang's birth), and he obviously fostered a love of music in his children, if by no other method than its constant presence in their house. He was an exceptional music teacher, who taught all other subjects in the Mozart household, as well. Nannerl and Wolfgang never attended school outside their home.

A clavier is the keyboard of a musical instrument. In some cases, it refers to a particular early keyboard instrument, or it can be used to indicate other instruments with keyboards, including the clavichord, the harpsichord, or the piano. The piano actually became Wolfgang's favorite instrument, and it was used for his

most personal expressions in music.[7] At the time of Mozart's death, his most expensive possessions were a pool table and a walnut piano.[8]

Page 17 – People declared that Wolfgang's ears were "magically sensitive," and that he could tell the pitch of an instrument to the eighth of a tone before he could even read.[9]

Page 20 – Wolfgang would amuse himself with sums for hours on end. When he was thirteen, he wrote to Nannerl asking her to send a copy of her rules of arithmetic because he had lost his own and was forgetting his mathematical tables. He also asked for any other arithmetic "examples" she could send to entertain him.[10] Playing with figures remained a hobby all his life. He even took up the popular problem of "composing minuets 'mechanically,' by putting two-measure melodic fragments together in any order."[11]

Page 21 – Wolfgang seemed to be born to create music. He rarely rested from composing, from the age of four until his death at thirty-five.[12] "Mozart did not choose to become a musician; music was born in him."[13]

A minuet is a French dance in triple meter (three beats per measure) that was popular from the mid-17th century to the end of the 18th century.

Page 22 – Wolfgang's ability to write music neatly improved with age. Most of the time, his music was already completed mentally before he would even put pen to paper.[14] He also could write pieces while visiting with friends, playing pool, or eating a meal.[15] "Composing is my one joy and passion," Wolfgang once wrote his wife.[16] It's interesting that he often used various colors of ink in writing his music. The most difficult passages were inked in bright blue.[17]

Page 23 – Herr Johann Andreas Schachtner was a trumpeter in the archbishop's court and a dear friend of the family. In 1792, Schachtner wrote Nannerl that Wolfgang's delicate and refined ear was horrified by the playing of a horn alone, so much so that "merely holding a horn toward him terrified him as much as if it had been a loaded pistol. His father wished to overcome this childish alarm, and ordered me once, in spite of his entreaties, to blow toward [Wolfgang]; but, oh! that I had not been induced to do it. Wolfgang no sooner heard the clanging sound than he turned pale and would have fallen into convulsions, had I not instantly desisted."[18]

Page 24 – Leopold's influence helped Wolfgang excel as a musician, but it also helped him achieve the character and greatness he displayed throughout most of his life.[19] No wonder Wolfgang's motto was, "Next to God comes Papa."

Chapter 2 – A Journey to Munich (1762)

Reading Comprehension Questions

1. How did Father Mozart, Nannerl, and Wolfgang entertain each other in the coach on the way to Munich?
   • They told funny stories and sang silly tunes, p. 28.
2. For which royal person were Nannerl and Wolfgang invited to play?
   • Prince Joseph, p. 30.
3. When the Mozart children gave concerts for the people of Munich during their three-week visit, what was the response they received?
   • Applause, praise, gifts, cheers, or amazement, p. 31.
4. In this chapter, what new instrument did Wolfgang prove he could play — self-taught? (He demonstrated this ability when Herr Schachtner, Herr Wentzel, and his father began to rehearse new trios.)
   • Violin, p. 34.
5. Why was Leopold crying at the end of this chapter?
   • He was astounded by Wolfgang's musical ability, p. 36.

Character Qualities

Family-Oriented – Leopold attended to and entertained his children on the coach ride to Munich (p. 27, 28). They were also glad to be reunited as a family at the month's end (p. 32).

Wit and Sense of Humor (p. 28) – The silly little song on this page hints at Wolfgang's love for laughter. Wolfgang had a lively disposition and fun-loving nature, which he is said to have received from his mother.[20] He had difficulty keeping still and was fond of jokes, games, dancing, masquerade balls, and singing.

Hard-working (p. 32) – While the children were highly praised and had great successes on this concert tour, they were willing to practice harder so they could play even better in the future.

Creativity (p. 33) – Wolfgang composed the first of his many minuets at age five. It was also incredible that he taught himself how to play the violin — especially the difficult parts of the first violin music (pp. 35, 36).

Tidbits of Interest

Page 27 – Wolfgang was not yet six when they left for Munich. Wolfgang was on one musical tour or another for over half his life![21]

Page 28 – Munich is the capital of Bavaria, which is a state in southern Germany, right along the Austrian border.

Page 30 – The Mozart children played for Prince Joseph, who was the court elector of Bavaria. His full title was Elector Maximilian Joseph III, and he was prince from 1745–1777. He was very influential in developing opera as a courtly entertainment in Bavaria.

Pages 34, 35 – When the men were practicing the new trios, Herr Wentzel played first violin (the hardest music in a composition); Herr Schachtner played second violin (a supporting, usually harmonizing role in music); and Leopold accompanied with a bass violin. Once again, we know about this event because Herr Schachtner wrote a detailed letter to Nannerl about that astonishing day and about the men's amazement at Wolfgang's natural talent with the violin.

Chapter 3 – They Play for the Queen (1762)

Reading Comprehension Questions

1. To what city were the Mozarts headed on a tour at the beginning of this chapter?
   • Vienna, p. 39.

2. In addition to Father Mozart, which family member accompanied the children on this trip?
   • Mother Mozart, p. 39.

3. When the Mozarts stopped in towns and inns along the way to Vienna, what did the children give?
   • Concerts — which were warmly received and praised, p. 41.

4. Do you remember how long it took the family to get to Vienna by coach on the rough, bumpy roads?
   • Almost four weeks…nearly an entire month, p. 42.

5. How did the Mozarts get through the customs house without having to pay duties on all the gifts they had received along the way?
   • Wolfgang entertained the customs officials who were so awed by the music of this small boy that they forgot all about the duties and let the Mozarts pass through, p. 42.

6. Among the invitations they received from nobles in Vienna, the children were finally asked to play for whom at Schönbrunn castle?
   • King Francis and Queen Maria Theresa, p. 43.

7. Can you supply proof that Wolfgang was not intimidated by or scared of the king and queen?
   • Wolfgang sat on the queen's lap and kissed her; he played with their children; he allowed the king to sit right next to his clavier while he played; and he performed one-finger and "blind" fingering tricks at the clavier for the king, pp. 44–46.

8. Why did Wolfgang "propose" to the young princess, Marie Antoinette?
   • She helped him up when he fell on the polished court floors, p. 46. Her kindness moved him deeply, p. 47.

9. What gifts did the children receive from Queen Maria Theresa?
   • Very elegant hand-me-downs...court clothes her own children had worn, p. 48.
10. What illness did Wolfgang endure toward the end of this tour?
   • Scarlet fever, p. 49.

Character Qualities

Family-Oriented (p. 39) – The whole family went on this bumpy trip to Vienna. Mother Mozart cared for Wolfgang when he became ill with scarlet fever, p. 49. Leopold decided to return to Salzburg for the sake of the health of his children (p. 50).

Humility (p. 41) – The children were unspoiled by all the praise and gifts they received. Nannerl was not jealous of Wolfgang's success and the attentions paid to him during concerts (p. 44). And they loved their good little home better than any king's palace (p. 50).

Playful (p. 44) – Don't you wish you could have seen Queen Maria Theresa's response to Wolfgang's springing into her lap and kissing her at their first meeting? Wolfgang played with the royal children and even played some musical "tricks" for the king (pp. 44, 45).

Kindness (pp. 46, 47) – Wolfgang was attracted to Marie Antoinette because of her kindness when he tripped and fell on the polished floor. The children were also kind in performing concerts for the townsfolk along the way to Vienna (p. 41).

Tidbits of Interest

Page 39 – Vienna is the capital of Austria, and it was the capital of the Austrian *empire* during the reign of the royal Hapsburg family (of whom Maria Theresa was a member).

Page 41 – Wolfgang and Nannerl remained remarkably unspoiled in the midst of all the attention they received.[22] In fact, Leopold once wrote Wolfgang, reminding him, "[A]s a boy you were so extraordinarily modest that you used to weep when people praised you overmuch."[23]

Page 42 – The Danube River is over 1,700 miles long, flowing from Germany through 200 miles of Austria. Ninety-six percent of Austria's land is drained by its rivers and tributaries. Castles and abbeys are perched all along the

Danube's banks, and it flows right through the city of Vienna.

Page 43 – King Francis I and Queen Maria Theresa were of the Hapsburg royal family. Maria Theresa was considered one of 18th-century Europe's most capable rulers (ruling Austria, Hungary, and Bohemia from 1740–1780). Their palace, Schönbrunn Palace, was the Hapsburg's showcase for wealth and architectural greatness.

Empress Maria Theresa apparently had a lovely voice and even appeared in an opera at age seven.[24] She had sixteen children, several of whom played significant roles in history, including Joseph II and Leopold II, who later became emperors of Austria. She began financial, educational, and agricultural reforms that strengthened Austria's economy and resources. Her son, Joseph II, co-ruled with her from 1765 through 1780, and then continued her positive reforms through 1790. He abolished serfdom, allowed freedom of the press, and stood up to the pope on issues of religious equality. Joseph II is credited with preventing the same kind of revolution in Austria that France experienced in the late 1700s — the revolution that cost his sister, Marie Antoinette, her head.

Page 46 – Georg Christoph Wagenseil was the Hapsburg family's court composer and music teacher from 1739 until his death in 1777. Wagenseil's compositions would have been very familiar to the Mozart children. An interesting sidelight is that one of Wagenseil's pupils went on to teach Ludwig van Beethoven.

Page 46 – One of the princesses Wolfgang met was Marie Antoinette, who was only two months older than Wolfgang.[25] Marie Antoinette married King Louis XVI of France. During the tumultuous months before and during the French Revolution, the people of France criticized her for her extravagance. It is alleged that she once replied, when told that the people had no bread to eat, "Let them eat cake!" In 1792, she secretly tried negotiating help from her imperial brother, Leopold II, in Austria, but the rioting revolutionaries overthrew the French monarchy. After a year in prison, this once kindly princess was tried and guillotined during the infamous "Reign of Terror."

Page 48 – A portrait was later painted of both of the Mozart children in those gift clothes from the Queen, so the coloring and designs are carefully documented in art. Wolfgang was very concerned about his appearance — fussing over his clothes, choosing elegant fashions as he grew older, and being very particular about how his hair looked.[26] It was difficult to work on the young composer's hair, however, because he would suddenly flit from his grooming chair to the keyboard to note a musical idea — with his barber in hot pursuit.[27]

Pages 48, 49 – Wolfgang had an exhausting childhood with a wearying schedule of concerts, fatiguing travel conditions, and exciting public appearances. Physical exhaustion would make anyone more susceptible to diseases such as scarlet fever, which is an acutely contagious disease that has symptoms of fever, a sore throat, and a red rash. It is caused by streptococci bacteria.

Page 51 – A common thought in most biographies about Wolfgang's life is that he was an affectionate lad who was eager to please. In spite of his illness and the physical toll such concerts took on him, Wolfgang was eager to do more concerts.

Page 52 – An allegro is a composition or a movement in a composition set in allegro tempo. *Allegro* is an Italian word meaning something done in a brisk and lively manner.

Chapter 4 – Visits to Royal Palaces
(1763 – 1766)

Reading Comprehension Questions

1. As the chapter began, the Mozart children were preparing to start a concert on a warm night in Frankfurt. Do you recall what costumes they were wearing?

    • The royal costumes from Queen Maria Theresa, p. 55.

2. This concert tour had many stops along the way — so many that it took them five months to reach which gay city along the River Seine in France?

    • Paris, p. 61.

3. What were some of the unique features of the king's palace at Versailles, near Paris?

    • Glittering lights, crystal chandeliers, rare tapestries, and bright ceiling paintings, p. 62.

4. King Louis XV, ruler at this time, was so impressed by the children that he even allowed Wolfgang to play on which instrument in the royal chapel?

    • The gilded organ (which means it was covered with a thin layer of gold), p. 62.

5. Their next visit on the tour was to a city across the English Channel. What was the city, and what was their reception there?

    • They visited London, where they were greeted even more cordially and successfully than in Paris, p. 63.

6. Queen Charlotte's music master in London was the son of a famous composer. Can you remember the master's name, or at least the last name of his family?

    • Johann Christian Bach, p. 65.

7. Leopold became ill and the children had to stop doing something for several weeks. (Most of you wouldn't object to this "silencing" demand.) What did they temporarily stop doing?

    • Practicing their music so that the house would be quiet for Leopold's recovery process, p. 67.

8. What did Wolfgang write during this sentence of musical silence?
    • His first symphony, at age eight, p. 67.
9. The Prince of Orange and Princess Caroline invited the Mozart children to visit them in what region?
    • Holland, p. 72.
10. How long did this entire concert tour last?
    • Three years, p. 73.

Character Qualities

Family-Oriented – This chapter describes a three-year concert tour they took as a family. They enjoyed family walks together (p. 65). And Wolfgang enjoyed having Nannerl nearby while he composed his symphony (p. 67).

Generous – Wolfgang gave long concerts because he loved music and wanted to please the people (p. 57). The children also played equally generously for royalty and common townsfolk alike (p. 72.)

Gracious (p. 72) – Nannerl and Wolfgang delighted everyone with their gracious ways. The praise that they received from listeners all over Europe and England, particularly from nobility, did not change how they treated those around them.

Tidbits of Interest

Page 57 – The people of Frankfurt hailed Wolfgang as a "wonder child." Both Wolfgang and Nannerl were dubbed *Wunderkinder*, the German word meaning "wonder children," because of their remarkable musical talents. Wolfgang also became known as the most kissed little boy in Europe during these musical tours.[28]

Page 58 – When they were in Heidelberg, Wolfgang was allowed to play the organ. The organ is a keyboard instrument in which sound is produced by air passing through pipes of varying size and construction to give a wide variety of pitches and timbres. In Wolfgang's time, bellows attached to foot pedals were the means of forcing air through the pipes of the organ. It is incredible that a boy of seven could "man" the bellows and play lovely music after only the second attempt of playing this instrument in his short lifetime!

Pages 60, 61 – This concert tour covered cities in Austria, Germany, Belgium, France, England, Holland (a province within the Netherlands), and Switzerland. The River Seine (pronounced \sane\ or \sen\) is a river in France that flows through Paris, northwest toward the English Channel.

Page 62 – King Louis XIV (the "Sun King") built the Palace of Versailles (pronounced \ver-sigh\) in the 17th century, and it was an enormous complex that housed some 5,000 aristocrats, ministers, servants, and royal family members. Thirty-six-thousand workers labored for almost thirty years on the palace. It was lavishly decorated and became the masterpiece of formal grandeur showing the glory of France. It also became the palatial ideal throughout Europe and the Americas for many decades after its construction. One hall, known as the Hall of Mirrors, had numerous mirrors to reflect candlelight, and the "sparkle of the crystal chandeliers," which amazed visitors like the Mozart children.

Nannerl and Wolfgang played for King Louis XV and his queen, Princess Marie Leszczynska of Poland. Under his poor leadership — politically and morally — the crown's power

Ⓐ SALON: THE PETIT TRIANON : VERSAILLES

declined, and Parlement (the chief judicial body under the ancient regime) gained power. He died a king hated by his subjects, and his excesses fostered the events that led to the French Revolution during his grandson's reign (King Louis XVI, the last French king).

Page 63 – The white cliffs of Dover are famous the world over. They are cliffs of soft, white chalk standing out against the horizon of the English Channel. The narrowest point across the channel is the twenty miles from Calais, France, to Dover, England, so Dover oversees one of the busiest seaways in the world.

The children's reputation had preceded them to England, and they were well received by the British. Advertisements for their concerts promised that "lovers of music, and all those who find some pleasure in extraordinary things" would be astounded "by the incredible dexterity of a girl of twelve and a boy of seven who astonished the Electoral Courts of Saxony, Bavaria, the Palatinate, and His Imperial and Royal Majesty during a four months' visit to Vienna."[29]

Page 64 – The guards at the royal residence mentioned in this chapter were Yeoman Warders, or Beefeaters (a nickname implying an overfed servant), who wore red and gold uniforms designed in the 16th century. The palace was Buckingham Palace, which had been newly acquired by King George III. He liked Buckingham House, and wanted a London residence, so he bought it in 1762, for £28,000. He renamed it Queen's House and gave it to his wife, Charlotte. Many of their fifteen children were born at the house.

Page 65 – The rulers of England at this time were King George III and Queen Charlotte. King George was only twenty-seven at the time, and his bride was only twenty-one. This is the same King George III to whom the colonists sent the Declaration of Independence, believing he was willfully infringing on their rights in order to establish an absolute tyranny over the colonies. Whatever his political style, he was a king who appreciated the musical styles of Georg Frideric Handel (who had been the British court composer from 1714 to 1759) and Johann Sebastian Bach. The influence of Bach's music in the royal court was undoubtedly enhanced by the fact that the current music master for the imperial family was Bach's youngest son, Johann Christian Bach. J.C. Bach wrote some fifty symphonies, and his musical works became the prototypes of the Classical style that Mozart followed in his own works. The music master introduced Mozart to the spirit of Italian music, which Bach admired for its form and beauty.[30] Music in the classical style has qualities associated with the art of ancient Greece and Rome, such as a focus on balance, symmetry, logic, and the natural expression of feeling — as opposed to technically complex or overwrought expressions. The Classical Period (1750 – 1820) was not so much a period of invention as one of development and perfection.

Queen Charlotte was apparently a musician of some note, or was at least unafraid of singing in public. Imagine being eight years old and accompanying a queen as she sings! Wolfgang went on to write several sonatas *for* Queen Charlotte.

Page 67 – Wolfgang continued to demonstrate his talents as a child prodigy (a child who is inexplicably and extraordinarily marvelous in some deed or accomplishment) by writing a symphony while Leopold was ill. It's interesting that he asked Nannerl to remind him to give the horns plenty of work because the exceptionally good London trumpeters impressed him.[31] (He apparently overcame his fear of horns as he aged.) A symphony, incidentally, is a large, complex composition for a *full* orchestra.

Page 68 – Throughout Mozart's career, he often received gifts rather than money for his musical compositions and concerts. As a child, this trend may not have been much of a concern, but as he matured and married, imperial dignity, jeweled boxes, and special costumes did not help pay the rent.[32] Yet, until his death, Mozart composed for the love of music, not for financial reward or man's acclaim. Some of his last and greatest symphonies, for example, were written without any promise of commission, or even the promise of an upcoming performance of those works.[33]

Page 69 – A sonata is a work composed for instruments, and it has three or four movements that differ in rhythm and mood but are related in key.

Page 70 – Their temporary move as a family to Chelsea (for the sake of Leopold's health) allowed Wolfgang to be outdoors. He enjoyed composing in gardens with birds around him.[34]

Page 71 – A waltz is music suitable for waltzing. (Don't you love those kinds of definitions?) Actually, a waltz is a gliding dance done to music having three beats per measure. Truly, this song *does* "sparkles" with fun. Mozart believed that all music should bring delight to the listener. Some critics call Mozart's gentleness and musical lightness a weakness in his music, and yet more recordings of Mozart's music are bought today than of any other composer's works.[35]

Page 72 – The Mozarts were in England for fifteen months, and it remained a country dear to Wolfgang's heart.[36] Before leaving for Holland, he underwent a "scientific examination" by a lawyer and musician named Daines Barrington. Some people were claiming that Wolfgang was a cheat (with his father writing the music, but crediting Wolfgang with the works), or that he was a man pretending to be a boy. In order to prove or disprove these claims, Barrington tested Wolfgang by observing him for several hours and reporting his observations in the *Philosophical Transactions* publication. Mr. Barrington recorded that Wolfgang was like any other boy of nine, in many ways — chasing cats, instead of playing the piano during practice hours, for instance.[37] Wolfgang also proved his musical genius by playing any difficult piece Barrington handed him and by writing a complicated composition before Barrington's eyes. These scientific tests put an end to the horrible rumors regarding Wolfgang's abilities.

The Prince of Orange, William V, was only seventeen years old, and Princess Caroline was his sister. The Mozart children played for these young royals at The Hague in 1765. The Hague is a city in the province of South Holland (in southwestern

Netherlands), and it is the seat of Netherlands' government. Holland, by the way, is a historic region in the northwest Netherlands, with Amsterdam as its capital. The term *Holland* is sometimes used to represent all of the Netherlands, but this is an incorrect labeling. Holland only makes up two of the twelve provinces that are unified as the Netherlands. All Netherlanders are *Dutch*, though.

Page 73 – While they were in Holland, Nannerl came down with a severe illness in September — to the point that Leopold feared she would die. Wolfgang also came down with a fever and did not feel like composing again until January 1766.[38]

On their way home to Salzburg, they traveled through France and Switzerland. In France they presented concerts in Paris, Versailles, Dijon, and Lyons; then in Switzerland they appeared in Geneva, Lausanne, Berne, and Zürich. They traveled through the Alps to return to Salzburg, arriving by November of 1766. This tour lasted for three years! In his short thirty-five-year lifespan, Wolfgang spent the equivalent of fourteen years on concert tours throughout Europe.[39]

Page 74 – Wolfgang declared that the canary still sang in the key of G. Wolfgang had perfect pitch, which is the ability to sing or name a note requested or heard. (It's also called absolute pitch.) Advertisements for the Mozarts' concerts even highlighted his ability to name all notes played at a distance, "singly or in chords," and "on the harpsichord, bells, glass, or clock."[40]

Chapter 5 – The Wonder Boy Grows Up
(1769 – 1791)

Reading Comprehension Questions

1. What new form of musical stories was Wolfgang beginning to compose in his pre-teen and teen years?
    • Opera, p. 79.

2. Explain what happened during Easter Week at the Sistine Chapel in Rome, according to this chapter.
    • Mozart memorized a special choral piece that was only to be seen by those taking part in the Easter service. Wolfgang wrote out his memorized copy, but it was against the pope's rules to possess a copy. However, instead of punishing Wolfgang, the pope presented him with the honor of the Order of the Golden Spur to recognize his rare talent. pp. 79–82.

3. When Wolfgang returned to Salzburg from his Italian tours, he became the court organist and concert master for whom?
    • The Archbishop of Salzburg, p. 83.

4. There was one thing Mozart never stopped doing from age five to his death. What was it?
    • Yes, breathing is a correct answer, but for this chapter the answer we were hoping to receive was *composing*, p. 83.

5. Why do you think Wolfgang could speak several different languages so well?
    • Because he had visited so many different countries in his travels and tours, p. 85.

6. Do you recall the name of Wolfgang's wife? And who was one of his dearest friends who was a fellow composer of note (no pun intended)?
    • Constance was his wife, and his notable friend was the composer Haydn, p. 85.

7. What was Wolfgang's comment or vision for the future when he heard the young Beethoven play the clavier?
    • Paraphrased: "Keep an eye on this man; he'll make a noise in the world some day," p. 86.

8. Why was the first performance of Wolfgang's opera *Don Giovanni* a little late in starting?
   • Copies of his overture, written in two hours on the day of the performance itself, were still being made for the orchestra, pp. 87, 88.
9. Can you name one of the other two operas that are mentioned in this chapter as among Wolfgang's greatest compositions?
   • *The Marriage of Figaro*, p. 86, and *The Magic Flute*, p. 90.

Character Qualities

Attentive (p. 78) – He wrote Nannerl while they were apart. He memorized the whole papal music composition in Rome during one service (pp. 79–81). He recognized and attended to talent in others, such as in Beethoven (p. 86).

Industrious (p. 83) – Wolfgang never stopped composing, even in the midst of court music duties, concert tours, giving lessons, and so forth. He wrote three operas in a short span of time.

Learned (p. 78) – He spent hours studying and writing each day. He was educated by his father in other academic areas, as well. He could speak several languages fluently (p. 85).

Friendliness (p. 85) – Wolfgang's friendships were deep, especially his one with Joseph Haydn, in whose honor he wrote six quartets.

Perseverance (p. 86) – Though Wolfgang's days were not always happy or struggle-free, he continued to work on his music. He tried to stay awake all night to finish the overture for *Don Giovanni*, but he ended up completing the work in a remarkable two hours of musical perseverance on the day of the opera's first performance (pp. 86, 87).

Joyful (p. 91) – His music is pure, beautiful, and filled with joy — for an entire world.

Tidbits of Interest

Page 77 – Four years before this chapter's opening scene, Wolfgang fell ill with smallpox on a trip to Vienna. Smallpox is an acute contagious disease that is now almost completely eradicated in the world. It causes skin blisters, or pustules, that are filled with pus. These blisters dry up, slough off, and leave pocked scars on the skin. It is believed that the fever accompanying this illness caused kidney damage in Wolfgang, and precipitated his early death at the age of thirty-five. Wolfgang was scarred from the smallpox and had yellowish skin with bulging blue eyes (more hints at possible kidney failure). He became very ill again in 1784, when it is thought one kidney failed him entirely.

Page 78 – Nannerl retired from concert tours, but she and Wolfgang remained dear siblings their whole lives. "[I] am ever your unalterably attached and loving brother" is a sample of Wolfgang's farewells in his letters to her.[41] Marianne continued to teach music all her life. She married a magistrate in 1784, had three children, and lived until 1829.[42]

Leopold Mozart devoted 1770–1773 as a time of travel and study in Italy so that Wolfgang could study, absorb, observe, and learn from the music and masters of the region.[43]

Pages 79–81 – A papal decree protected Gregorio Allegri's *Miserere*, sung by the Papal Choir only during Holy Week. (*Miserere* is Latin for "have mercy.") A special guard was even established to keep the manuscript from being seen, copied, or used anywhere else, and those found in possession of a copy were immediately punished by excommunication from the Catholic church.[44] Nevertheless, Pope Clement XIV showed mercy, and perhaps a slight sense of humor, by ignoring the punishment of excommunication, and instead he bestowed on Wolfgang (at age fourteen) the honor of the Order of the Golden Spur. This Order was an honorary knighthood given by the pope, but requiring no specific obligations — particularly none of a martial or military nature.

Page 81 – Wolfgang didn't even notice the ceiling art in the Sistine Chapel because he so enthralled by the music. Michelangelo Buonarroti, the famous Italian artist and sculptor, spent four years (1508–1512) painting the ceiling and vault of the chapel with intricate decorations that include scenes from the Book of Genesis, the prophets, and ancestors of Christ.

Page 83 – Wolfgang returned to Salzburg for a six-year stay, working in the court of a new archbishop, Hieronymus Colloredo. Colloredo was not as well-disposed to his young music master as Archbishop Schrattenbach had been during his childhood. Once, in a fit of rage, Collerodo even had Wolfgang physically kicked down the steps of the cathedral.

Page 85 – Wolfgang learned fifteen languages in all his travels.[45] He married Constance Weber in 1782, a young lady eight years younger than himself, but who outlived him by fifty years.[46] They had a steadfast and loving marriage, in spite of many hardships they endured. Constance was a faithful helpmeet (living up to her name) who encouraged Wolfgang in his composing, and shared six children with him — though only two lived to adulthood: Karl Thomas (1784–1858) and Franz Xaver (1791–1844). Wolfgang and Constance moved twelve times in their nine years of marriage, and they always seemed to be scrabbling for the needed finances.[47] At one point some friends came to visit the Mozarts only to find them dancing in one of the rooms during the middle of the day. Wolfgang explained that they had run out of firewood, and they were dancing to stay warm! In spite of these hardships, Wolfgang's last ten years of compositions — during his marriage – are among his most famous and artistically beautiful.

Franz Joseph Haydn (1732–1809) was twenty-four years older than Wolfgang, but they became close friends. They were fellow Austrian composers who first met each other in 1782, yet they never experienced any musical rivalry or jealousy between them. In fact, they stimulated each other, and it is said that "the contemporary master from whom Mozart learned most, after Johann Christian Bach, was the elder of the brothers Haydn — Joseph Haydn."[48] Haydn's adventurous compositions influenced

Mozart's creativity, and Wolfgang dedicated six string quartet pieces to his older friend. When Haydn first heard these six quartets, he turned to Wolfgang's father and proclaimed, "Before God and as an honest man, I tell you that your son is the greatest composer known to me either in person or by name."[49]

Page 86 – Although Wolfgang could not take Ludwig van Beethoven on as a student at the point that Beethoven came to see him, Wolfgang recognized the incredible talent in this young German musician. In 1826, years after Mozart's death, Beethoven stated, "I have always reckoned myself among the greatest venerators [admirers] of Mozart, and I shall remain so until my last breath."[50]

Opera is a musical drama in which the performers sing most or all of their lines, and the music is just as important as the words. Opera was considered the premier style of music to write in the 18th century. "When a composer was asked to write an opera, he knew he had reached the top."[51] Wolfgang wrote his first opera at age twelve, and it was performed in Milan when he was only fourteen. His favorite style of operas to write was comic operas. (That matches his playful, cheerful personality, does it not?)

The Marriage of Figaro, written in 1786, caused a tremendous sensation in Prague, the capital city in what is now the Czech Republic. Prague is famous for its opera houses, theaters, and puppet theaters, and *Figaro* played to a packed house each performance. Wolfgang wrote of its overwhelming success in Prague: "[For] here nothing is talked about but 'Figaro,' nothing played but 'Figaro,' nothing whistled or sung but 'Figaro,' no opera so crowded as 'Figaro,' nothing but 'Figaro,' — very flattering to me, certainly."[52]

Wolfgang's next opera, *Don Giovanni,* was written just a few months after his father's death in 1787. Action appears to have been Wolfgang's remedy for discouragement.[53] Instead of succumbing to depression, or resting on his laurels as a child prodigy, Wolfgang constantly tried new and innovative compositions to ease his sense of loss or distress. Wolfgang could write music more quickly than almost any other composer in history, but he sometimes procrastinated, which often necessitated late-night composing sessions. Constance was known to stay awake with Wolfgang to tell him stories of Aladdin and Cinderella,[54] share jokes with him, and bring him his favorite punch while he composed.[55]

Page 91 – Sadly, Wolfgang died at only thirty-five years of age. He was in physical misery with complications most historians believe were related to kidney failure, malnutrition, and exhaustion.[56] He died on December 5, 1791, dictating another composition from his bed. Mozart composed over six hundred pieces of an amazing variety: quartets, concertos, sonatas, divertimentos, serenades, symphonies, church music, and operas.[57] If one were to listen to all Mozart's works in a row, it would take eight and a half days (202 hours)![58]

No one is certain where Johannes Chrysostomus Wolfgangus Theophilus Mozart was buried in Vienna. At his death, Wolfgang only had 38 dollars' worth of worldly goods, not nearly enough for a funeral.[59] So a friend and musical admirer paid for his burial — but only in a pauper's grave. As the coffin was taken into the cemetery, a thunderstorm broke forth and caused the escorting mourners to run for shelter. Only the gravediggers were present when the body of this musical genius was lowered in an unmarked grave. (Even Constance was not present; she had just had a son a few months before, and she was so distraught by Wolfgang's death that she was under a doctor's care at the time of the funeral.) The graveyard caretaker had no recollection of where the renowned composer had been buried when Constance later questioned the caretaker about her husband's grave.

Wolfgang Mozart was a composer of indefatigable enthusiasm, action, and spirit. When an emperor once told Wolfgang that his music had too many notes, Mozart retorted, "Just as many notes as are necessary, Your Majesty."[60] Perhaps that is what could be said about Mozart's life: "Just as many notes as are necessary…" and just as many days as were necessary to compose music that has brought delight for decades to listeners around the world.

Endnotes

[1] Roland Vernon, *Introducing Mozart* (London: Belitha Press Limited, 1996), 6.

[2] Patrick Kavanaugh, *The Spiritual Lives of the Great Composers* (Grand Rapids, MI: Zondervan, 1996), 47.

[3] Alfred Einstein, *Mozart, His Character, His Work* (London: Oxford University Press, 1945), 78.

[4] Kathleen Krull, *Lives of the Musicians: Good Times, Bad Times* (San Diego, CA: Harcourt, Inc., 2002), 20.

[5] Peggy Woodford, *Mozart* (London: Omnibus Press, 1990), 11.

[6] Einstein, *Mozart*, 13.

[7] Ibid., 55.

[8] Krull, *Lives of the Musicians*, 23.

[9] Henry Thomas and Dana Lee Thomas, *Living Biographies of Great Composers* (Garden City, NY: Nelson Doubleday, Inc., 1940), 53.

[10] Louis Biancolli, *The Mozart Handbook* (Cleveland, OH: The World Publishing Company, 1954), 12.

[11] Einstein, *Mozart*, 25.

[12] Jane Stuart Smith and Betty Carlson, *The Gift of Music: Great Composers and Their Influence* (Wheaton: IL: Crossway Books, 1995), 52.

[13] Rachel Isadora, *Young Mozart* (New York: Viking, 1997), 29.

[14] Kavanaugh, *The Spiritual Lives of the Great Composers*, 46.

[15] Krull, *Lives of the Musicians*, 21.

[16] Smith and Carlson, *The Gift of Music*, 52.

[17] Ibid., 55.

[18] Einstein, *Mozart*, 151.

[19] Smith and Carlson, *The Gift of Music*, 53.

[20] Ibid.

[21] Ibid.

[22] Biancolli, *The Mozart Handbook*, 13.

[23] Einstein, *Mozart*, 28.

[24] Biancolli, *The Mozart Handbook*, 35.

[25] Ibid., 36.

[26] Krull, *Lives of the Musicians*, 20.

[27] Kavanaugh, *The Spiritual Lives of the Great Composers*, 46.

[28] Krull, *Lives of the Musicians*, 20.

[29] Ordentliche Wochenliche Franckfurter Frag-und Anzeigungs-Nachrichten, August 16, 1763. (Quoted from The Mozart Project website on November 21, 2004.)

[30] Smith and Carlson, *The Gift of Music*, 54.

[31] Biancolli, *The Mozart Handbook*, 45.

[32] Samuel Nisenson and William DeWitt, *Illustrated Minute Biographies* (New York: Grosset & Dunlap, 1953), 113.

[33] Kavanaugh, *The Spiritual Lives of the Great Composers*, 52.

[34] Smith and Carlson, *The Gift of Music*, 55.

[35] Krull, *Lives of the Musicians*, 23.

[36] Einstein, *Mozart*, 89.

[37] Catherine Brighton, *Mozart* (New York: Doubleday, 1990), 18.

[38] Biancolli, *The Mozart Handbook*, 49.

[39] Krull, *Lives of the Musicians*, 23.

[40] Kavanaugh, *The Spiritual Lives of the Great Composers*, 46.

[41] Lady Wallace, *The Letters of Wolfgang Amadeus Mozart* (Boston: Oliver Ditson & Co., no date given but sometime before 1877), 81.

[42] Brighton, *Mozart*, 24.

[43] Smith and Carlson, *The Gift of Music*, 54.

[44] Kavanaugh, *The Spiritual Lives of the Great Composers*, 45.

[45] Krull, *Lives of the Musicians*, 19.

[46] Vernon, *Introducing Mozart*, 18.

[47] Smith and Carlson, *The Gift of Music*, 56.

[48] Einstein, *Mozart*, 126.

[49] Smith and Carlson, *The Gift of Music*, 57.

[50] Kavanaugh, *The Spiritual Lives of the Great Composers*, 47.

[51] Vernon, *Introducing Mozart*, 11.

[52] Lady Wallace, *The Letters of Wolfgang Amadeus Mozart*, 218.

[53] Kavanaugh, *The Spiritual Lives of the Great Composers*, 52.

[54] Krull, *Lives of the Musicians*, 21.

[55] Kavanaugh, *The Spiritual Lives of the Great Composers*, 49.

[56] Biancolli, *The Mozart Handbook*, 31.

[57] Smith and Carlson, *The Gift of Music*, 57.

[58] Krull, *Lives of the Musicians*, 23.

[59] Thomas and Thomas, *Living Biographies of Great Composers*, 69.

[60] Ibid., 62.

Glossary of musical terms

Sonatina (p. 93) – A little sonata; simpler in structure and shorter in length than a sonata.

French Melody with Variation (pp. 94) – A variation involves repeating a theme but changing it by varying the melody, its rhythm, or its harmony, or by adding something to the original work.

Andante (pp. 96) – Coming from the Italian word meaning "walking," so the speed of this piece is at a walking pace, or a moderate pace.

Rondo (p. 97) – This form of music involves using a recurring theme between a series of different episodes, and it always starts with a cheerful or lively tune. It is also used for the final, rapid movement in some classical concertos or symphonies.

Bagatelle (pp. 98) – Literally meaning "a trifle." It is a short piece (usually for the piano) that is lighthearted in nature.

Presto (p. 100) – An Italian word meaning "quick."

Sonata (p. 101) – Instrumental music; generally in several movements that might involve one or more instruments that differ from each other in tempo and character. The sonata form has three sections in a movement: exposition of the main theme; development of that theme with rhythmic, melodic, or harmonic variations; and recapitulation, which serves to re-present the theme or themes of the original exposition.

Minuet (p. 102) – A triple-meter (three beats per measure) French dance that was popular from the mid-17th century to the end of the 18th century.

Allegretto (p. 107) – A slightly slower piece than an *allegro* (which is Italian for "cheerful and lively"). Neither an *allegretto* nor an *allegro* is as fast as a *presto*.

Ländler (pp. 116) – An Austrian country dance in slow meter with three beats per measure. It was the precursor of the waltz.

Secondo (pp. 116) – Second, or second player.

Primo (pp. 117) – First, or first player.

Minuetto (pp. 120) – The Italian word for "minuet."